Tending The Beloved:
Healing Wounds Into Scars
Featuring the S.C.A.R.s. Method®

Michelle Andrea Williams

To Laura,
Excited to
see what God
has in store –
Trusting!
Michelle A. Williams

Tending The Beloved: Healing Wounds Into Scars
Copyright © 2018 Michelle Andrea Williams

Cover Design by Michelle Andrea Williams with Lynn Eggleton
Cover Artwork by Brigitte Werner https://pixabay.com/en/users/werner22brigitte-5337/
Interior Artwork by Gordon Johnson https://pixabay.com/en/users/GDJ-1086657/
Edited by Caroline Anschutz

Printed in the United States of America

The content in this workbook is not intended to be a substitute for professional mental health or medical advice, diagnosis, or treatment. Always seek the advice of your physician or other qualified healthcare or mental health provider with any questions you may have regarding a medical or mental health condition.

ISBN-13: 978-0-9991702-2-9
ISBN-10: 0-9991702-2-8

For Deb, Dorie, Robin & Sherry

You, Lord, took up my case;
you redeemed my life.
Lamentations 3:58 NIV

CONTENTS

INTRODUCTION

After living with wounds for decades, I asked God to take over my life. What followed was a methodical plan to help me heal from deep-seeded wounds I sustained along the way. The journey has been challenging. Certain times called for unbridled faith and courage. I laid out the intimate story in my first book, "Finding My Damascus," to show others God has a plan for our sufficient healing.

Through God's direction, I took classes, went to therapy, and read books on skills I needed to learn to reach a level of sufficient healing. God led me to create this workbook to help those seeking His Divine Guidance and discover the path He has laid out for each of us to find healing. Through Jesus, with the aid of the Holy Spirit, the Helper given to us as a Guide, God has a healing plan for us all.

The journey was not easy, but in the end, the level of healing I experienced was worth the pain and hard work it took to achieve it. There were moments when faith was all I had because my resolve and courage failed me. I spent time reading scriptures to push through and move past barriers.

Each healing moment assured me of God's unfailing Love for us through His Son Jesus Christ, a personal, sacrificial, eternal Love that binds all wounds, heals all hurts, and provides us with the wholeness we so long for. We are created to Love God and receive Love from our Creator. The Love is relational and intentional, and beyond anything we could ever imagine – we are His Beloved Children.

I pray you find the path God has set for you. The journey may be bumpy and challenging but, with courage, faith and work, the path will lead you to the life God designed for you - one with Him through His Son and filled with peace, happiness, and the sufficient healing you deserve.

I wish you courage and resolve.
Michelle Andrea Williams

HOW TO USE THIS WORKBOOK

Tending The Beloved: Healing Wounds Into Scars is designed to offer us a chance to find deep-seeded wounds and heal them into scars using God's plan. We are each a unique creation; therefore the plan for our healing is also unique and tailored to our needs. The workbook is intended to be a tool in self-discovery and God-discovery to realize His plan to heal our wounds into scars.

When the body is injured, the process of healing begins immediately, but the complexity comes from underlying or unknown conditions – infection, malnourishment, and others. It's the *underlying* conditions that cause the wound to take much longer to heal. The body must repair itself through several phases – fight infection, grow new cells, knit together the tissue and bone – a simple description for a very complex method. Yet, once healing is complete, a scar remains – evidence showing injury once took place but no longer causes pain. A scar indicates sufficient healing. [1]

A similar process happens when we are subjected to emotional wounding. Fear and anxiety can stifle our healing and wrestling with emotions depletes our energy. Additionally, underlying conditions can hamper our emotional healing – depression, PTSD, mental health, physical health – these issues must be addressed by a trained professional. The process of healing requires courage and resolve to dig into our worst fears and deepest hurts. Our aim is to seek God's plan for our path to healing.

The workbook is designed to be used over and over to help us with large and small wounds to reach the healing we so deserve. Each chapter builds on the next to seek God's guidance. Our goal is to identify the wound, assess what it is doing to ourselves and those around us, and create a vision of a sufficiently healed version of ourselves and our lives. We will end with a plan of action based on what God has shown us through the course. The journey can be hard, yet most rewarding.

The chapters contain four sections created to help us focus on God's message and plan. Each is as important as the others in drawing out the deep wounds, examining each, and finding God's navigation through the healing process.

[1] - Physiology Of Wound Healing. T Hunt-H Hopf-Z Hussain - https://www.ncbi.nlm.nih.gov/pubmed/11074996

Meditation – Contemplative Prayer is a time to soften the mind, allowing our spirit to draw itself to God without life's demands or urgent requests for God's action interfering in the connection. It is a simple quietness, a focus on God's Presence, and a way to decompress from all the stresses we experience. Our aim is to commune with our Creator. There are several apps designed to aid in the contemplative prayer process. The one I use and recommend is Centering Prayer by Contemplative Outreach Ltd. It can be tailored to your preference, the length of time to meditate can be adjusted, and has no ads. You can visit the website for Contemplative Outreach and learn more about Centering Prayer. [2]

The Story portion of each chapter shares Jesus' teachings, actions, and words to offer us encouragement, direction, and discernment for our own lives. The stories are written based on the Gospels but in my own words with some comments and interjections. Those portions in quotations are directly from the NIV version of the Bible.

Jesus was the greatest storyteller and understood the human psychology of connecting with stories. Each one has a little twist to offer a different perspective on these age-old teachings. I hope you see, as I did, how God uses scripture to show us something new each time we read it – the mystery behind the story.

The Gospels share stories of Jesus tending the beloved children of God through every action, healing, and parable. Jesus is shown as radical, practical, loving and relentless in His pursuit of truth, healing, and grace. I hope the stories touch you as deeply and profoundly as they touched me.

The Lesson section offers us God's interactions with Old and New Testament characters and provide affirmation of Jesus' stories. I invite you to read the referenced scriptures in this section and hope it refines your view of God and offers a better way, His way, of looking at life, people, and ourselves.

---

[2] – Centering Prayer. (n.d.). Retrieved September 20, 2018, from
https://www.contemplativeoutreach.org/category/category/centering-prayer

The S.C.A.R.s. Method®, in Chapter 2, is a step by step process God revealed to me for working through issues and emotions and can be repeated as often as necessary. The practice is designed to Separate ourselves from the emotions and issues, Clarify what plan God has for us, Ask for help when needed, Rebuild ourselves and our lives to be more like He designed, and to
share our story with others to offer hope and encouragement only when we reach sufficient healing.

The Skill section offers creative ways to discover those life-skills God wants us to master to become sufficiently healed. References are used to deep-dive the skill and offer insight into building skills in our lives. The questions are designed to help us gain honesty and insight while allowing those deep hurts to surface and begin healing into scars.

Learning new skills requires practice, patience, and determination. Remember, if you will, learning to ride a bike or swimming or driving a car. Each required instruction, practice time, application, and relentless patience – in ourselves and sometimes from others. Once we mastered the new skill, it became second nature and our muscles and brain worked together like a well-oiled machine. God will show up and lead us to learn these new skills and aid us in achieving sufficient healing.

The Questions section has is made up of five questions pertaining to the chapter topic, skill or story. Each is to be completed in class sessions prior to writing in the journal. The answers may surprise us and hopefully will offer insight into our own thoughts and feelings.

The Journal Prompts are supplemental and designed to provide writing topics with each prompt aiming us to separate ourselves emotionally from a situation or event, gain clarity on God's path, discern questions needing answered, offer insight into rebuilding our lives, and connect with God. The journals should be private and sacred to honestly share our innermost thoughts and feelings. It is intended to be a two-way conversation with God in which we write how we feel, our thoughts, and concerns and then document what we think God is leading us to think or act on through prayer, scripture and meditation.

I recommend books covering various topics – setting boundaries, difficult conversations, gaining clarification, seeking therapy, and support. You will find the resources referenced throughout the workbook and listed in the Resources section. Please find those topics in which you need to further explore and invest in the proper learning to repair and allow God to heal your wounds into scars.

Before Beginning: The Rock of our Wounding

This is an exercise in *not* sharing our personal stories with others. Before beginning this course, find a large rock about the size of your hand. The rock represents the wounding we all carry. We hold on to the rock keeping it close until we can no longer bear the weight. To relieve our burden, we talk about our problems and worries with others including close friends, family members, or the lady in the checkout line – whoever will allow us to open up and hand over our rock. They bear it for us temporarily until the rock reappears since it was *passed off* to someone who is incapable of holding it for us – they have their own to hold. Everyone does.

It is important to have conversations about what worries us, but we need to be mindful of the motivation behind the discussion. Are we truly seeking advice from the listener? If so, are we taking the advice to help resolve our problems or wounding? Or are we offloading our pent-up pain for a temporary emotional relief? We have all done this *offloading of the rock* for others to hold only to have it mysteriously come back to us. Even when we receive the best advice, we may continue down the same path unable to let it go completely.

We will keep our story to ourselves during this course to focus the communication between us to the only One who will carry our burdens forever, Jesus Christ. Through Him, the burden is light, the yoke is easy, and we will truly find rest for our souls. (Matthew 11:29-30)

So, take let's take the rock of our wounding and lay it down. Sharing with others is the last thing we need to do until sufficient healing is achieved, and our story can be used to offer hope and encouragement to others. Sharing will be a testimony of faith for God's healing grace through Christ.

For Small Group Sessions, All Day or Two-Day Workshops:

This workbook can be used for small group studies and are best when each chapter is covered in a weekly or bi-weekly meet up. Allocate about an hour and half per session to have ample time to cover the story, lesson, skill, and questions. Journal prompts are designed for the class attendee to take home and use on their own.

The workbook also works well in a workshop setting in which participants have enough time to get through the material and answer the questions in all eight chapters. If an 8 to 10-hour day is too long, a two-day workshop is recommended.

Each chapter session should be about 30-45 min long with an additional 15-20 minutes for answering questions. Short breaks between each chapter is highly recommended to allow the participants to decompress and have some breathing room. Example: 5-10 min breaks twice in the morning, a 45 minute or so lunch then two more 5-10 min breaks in the afternoon.

Have local and church sponsored resources available prior to starting the small group or workshop. Examples include counseling services, support groups, mental health resources, etc. A prayer team, or prayer support, is a great supplement to workshops and small groups – give each participant the opportunity to ask for individual prayer with confidentiality and privacy.

Above all – ask God to lead you in how this workbook will be used in your group, church, community or conference. He has a plan and will reveal it to you.

I pray for those using this workbook and those leading classes and workshops. May God clearly guide you on His path to sufficient healing of each person's wounds into scars.

In Jesus' Service,
Michelle Andrea Williams

Tending The Beloved:
Healing Wounds Into Scars
Featuring the S.C.A.R.s Method

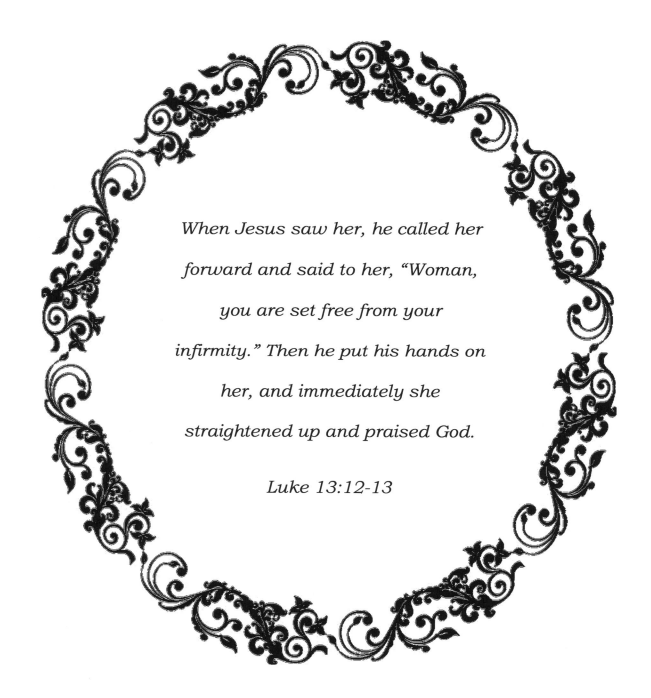

When Jesus saw her, he called her forward and said to her, "Woman, you are set free from your infirmity." Then he put his hands on her, and immediately she straightened up and praised God.

Luke 13:12-13

Chapter 1
Living with Wounds

MEDITATION – CONTEMPLATIVE PRAYER

Spend one minute in silence focusing on one word to draw our attention back to God, Christ, Love or another powerful word to connect our spirit with the Holy.

THE STORY: The Healing Pool

Thirty-eight years! Can we imagine living with an ailment or disability for thirty-eight years? In modern times, disabled people can lead similar lives to those of abled people with the resources available. Healing and treatment were not easily available for disabled and ill people 2,000 years ago. They had little choice.

John described the life of those with disabilities during that time through the story of the healing pool in the Book of John, Chapter 5. He tells us a great number of disabled people, those who were blind, crippled and paralyzed, would lie by the pool surrounded by colonnades near a gate in Jerusalem. An Angel would descend and stir the waters occasionally, after which, the first person to enter the water would be healed of whatever affliction they were living with. Of all the people near the healing pool, no one helped this ailing man into the waters. (John 5:2-4)

Jesus went to Jerusalem to attend one of the Jewish festivals held there and walked by the healing pool. Of the multitude of people by the pool, Jesus noticed the lame man who had been suffering for a long time. (John 5:1,6) We do not know the man's name, how old he was, or his life before the moment Jesus spotted him. We do know he suffered, he could not walk, and he had likely been by the pool waiting for his miracle for a long, long time.

Jesus did not ask him about the previous thirty-eight years, he only asked, "Do you want to get well?" (John 5:6) The man's response was evident of how he dealt with his disability. He responded, "Sir, I have no one to help me into the pool when the water is stirred. While I am trying to get in, someone else goes down ahead of me." (John 5:7)

Let's pause for moment and understand what this man's response means. *They won't let me in*, he complains. *It's all their fault. I am trying to get into the healing waters, but it is too hard. No one has enough compassion to help me.* The lame man was expecting the countless number of other incapacitated people to help *him* into the water for healing. His answer indicated this happened many times over.

How did Jesus respond? He ignored the man's complaining and gave a short, precise command. Jesus said to him, "Get up!" (John 5:7) *Get up*, not, *Oh, let Me help you into the stirred waters since no one else will.* The method of healing the man was seeking was unattainable from where he was, and he spent thirty-eight years suffering because of it. Jesus continued, "Get up! Pick up your mat and walk." Only then, when he heard the instructions God gave him through Jesus did he experience healing. And he did just as Jesus commanded, he picked up his mat and walked. (John 5:8-9)

The man sought unreachable healing – the wrong place, the wrong people, and the wrong method. He looked to suffering people for support. His neighbors were in no condition or mental state to help him find healing. It took Jesus' simple command, a plan laid out in front of him, which had nothing to do with how he had lived the last thirty-eight years. Was it so simple – to just pick up his mat and walk? Jesus said it was and when the lame man followed the instructions set out by the Son of God, he found the healing he longed for.

THE LESSON: God's Way
How many times have we floundered in our own pain, wounding, and hurt and made excuses that kept us from finding sufficient healing? Seeking the help of others in our lives may be futile since most people are dealing with their own unhealed wounds and can offer very little help. Living with wounds, emotional and physical, may require professional care. Just as a deep cut or broken bone

require the care of a physician, proper medical attention, so may the wounding we experience emotionally. Unless one in our own household is a licensed therapist, we need to seek help elsewhere.

God's plan for our emotional healing may be to seek professional help along with a retraining of our thoughts and views through scriptural lessons offered in the Bible. The question is, "Do we want to get well?" When we answer yes and stop making excuses, the plan to sufficient healing will be revealed. God is ready to help us, when we are ready to accept His help.

THE SKILL: Reverence for God

Jesus gave the lame man a command, "Get Up!" Imagine the man laying by the pool and looking at the Son of God. He could have turned to his previous thoughts, and aimed for the pool once again for healing, or, even worse, continued to seek help from those who could do nothing for him. Instead, he listened, he had reverence, he showed an honor and respect towards Jesus to follow the simple instructions he heard. His habit of incorrect thinking could have steered him to disregard the simplicity of the command and have no confidence in the weight of Jesus' words. He chose differently. He followed the plan and he was healed. (John 5:8)

Showing our own reverence for God is to open ourselves up to whatever instructions He has in store. Will the words be as simple as the ones given to the lame man? We always hope so, but we must show the respect and openness necessary to hear the message and the courage to follow the instructions. This requires listening and acting on what we believe God is guiding us to do.

Let us work through some of the incorrect views about our wounded self and see what God has to offer instead.

THE QUESTIONS:

1. What steps have you taken to help heal your emotional wounds?

_____

_____

_____

_____

_____

_____

_____

2. What has worked and what has not?

_____

_____

_____

_____

_____

_____

_____

3. What one thing do you believe God has shown you to achieve sufficient healing, but you have not had the courage on which to act?

_____

_____

_____

_____

_____

_____

4. What steps do you need to take to change your old way of thinking and be open to God's plan for healing?

_____

_____

_____

_____

_____

_____

_____

_____

5. Find one scripture giving you assurance God oversees your healing plan.

_____

_____

_____

_____

_____

_____

THE JOURNAL PROMPTS

Focus on one emotion you are having trouble with and write from "its" perspective. Name it as a character – fear, anxiety, anger, etc. Let it speak to you through a story or poem, or simply writing how it views you.

Write a descriptive view of your deepest wound, if you are ready, and explain how the injury occurred and what effects the wounds has had since.

Free write the expectations you have taking this course: expectations of yourself, expectations of God, and those supporting you.

Ask God a question about your wound and truly seek His answer through prayer and scripture. What does God have to say about your wound?

Chapter 2
Living With Scars

MEDITATION – CONTEMPLATIVE PRAYER

Spend two minutes in silence focusing on one word to draw our attention back to God, Christ, Love or another powerful word to connect our spirit with the Holy.

THE STORY: Thomas and Jesus

Scars have purpose. Once healing is sufficient, the scar reminds us the wound is no longer open, no longer hurts and is protected from infection. The wounded spot may never look as it did before the injury, but it is sufficiently healed. And every scar has a story. God gives us opportunities to join Him in a healing process that provides us with peace, hope, and assurance of His Love. Once we become sufficiently healed, sharing the stories of our scars provides hope and encouragement to others.

In the Book of John, Chapter 20, John shares with us the story of Thomas' nonbelief and how Jesus changed his mind. After the Resurrection, Jesus visited Thomas and the other disciples with the purpose of offering them a chance to believe. The disciples were behind locked doors for fear of someone from the Temple finding them. Thomas was not present when Jesus first appeared to the disciples. Jesus stood among the disciples and said, "Peace be with you!" He then showed the disciples His hands and side. The disciples were ecstatic to see Him. (John 20:19-20)

Later, the disciples told Thomas of their encounter with Jesus, but Thomas didn't believe them. "Unless I see the nail marks in his hands and put my finger where the nails were, and put my hand into his side, I will not believe." (John 20:24-25) Thomas would not take the disciples word for it, he had to see Jesus for himself and, the signs of the crucifixion – the remnants of the wounds.

A week later, Thomas was with the disciples in the same locked-up house when Jesus appeared in their midst and said, "Peace be with you." (John 20:26) Then Jesus showed Thomas what He has shown the other disciples the previous week, "Put your finger here; see my hands. Reach out your hand and put it into my side. Stop doubting and believe," Jesus instructed Thomas. (John 20:27) And what was Thomas' reaction? Thomas said to him, "My Lord and my God." (John 20:28) Belief, total and complete belief in the Son of God, the Messiah.

Jesus knew His nail marks and speared side had meaning and purpose – they told a story. The same Power of God that rose Jesus from the dead could have healed each mark, puncture, and gash. Jesus could have appeared unblemished, healed, as perfect as the day He was born, but God had bigger plans.

The marks remaining on Jesus' body after He rose from the dead served the purpose of offering a chance for the disciples to believe Jesus was who He said He was, the Messiah. The ten disciples believed because they saw first Jesus' hands and side. The disciples knew the Truth and conveyed the message to Thomas, but Thomas would not believe their story – he needed proof.

Let's dig a little deeper. Was Thomas the only one who had unbelief and doubts? He may not have been any different than the other disciples. If we look back, we can see Jesus understood this. Peter and the other disciples had a hard time believing Mary and the women on the day of Christ's Resurrection. (Luke 24:10-11) Peter still doubted even after he had declared Jesus was The Messiah (Mark 8:29). He had to race to the empty tomb to see for himself. Yet, he still left unsure and confused. (John 24:12) Would the other disciples have reacted the same as Thomas if they were not there the previous week? Jesus likely believed so, hence the reason for God leaving the marks on His Resurrected body.

Even more so, the disciples had undergone a traumatic time, full of grief, fear, hopelessness and disappointment. They went from a celebration during the Last Supper to Christ's arrest in the same evening. Within a day, their Leader was tried, convicted by church leadership, beaten, and crucified. They must have been horrified, fearing for their lives – hence the reason behind Peter denying even knowing Jesus – not once but three times, as Jesus foresaw. (Matthew

26:69-75) We understand why the disciples stayed behind locked doors. They must have felt abandoned, hopeless, and all they had endured was for nothing.

Jesus knew the disciples emotional and mental state. He knew they were fearful, hopeless and unbelieving. He had to enter their presence in a most unconventional way and show each one the marks on His Resurrected body to provide each with Peace, Hope, and Belief. Thomas was the last disciple to experience the Resurrected Jesus.

THE LESSON: God Has a Purpose

Jesus used the nail holes in His hands and the gash in His side to show all the disciples He was who He said He was – The Risen Messiah, the Son of God, the Christ. He used the marks as proof for those who struggled to believe, who were under so much emotional trauma that only clear, undeniable evidence would suffice. Jesus walked the earth between Resurrection and Ascension to continue to teach the disciples to do the work He had called each of them to do. God fulfilled His promise and purpose through Jesus' marks – the remnants of His wounds.

Jesus used stories throughout His ministry to teach others and understood stories have power. We can use our scars to teach others, offer hope, provide encouragement, and point to God's Grace. We must be at a place of sufficient healing with scars to point to instead of gaping wounds before we share our story. God wants us to tell the story. However, if we lay out the problem with no resolution, the story is incomplete and shows that our healing is incomplete. We have work to do. God leads us to heal our wounds into scars. Living with scars means the wounds neither hurt nor affect our daily lives negatively any longer. We are sufficiently healed.

THE SKILL: The S.C.A.R.s Method
SEPARATE

Separation requires a change from one's internal interests to another's or an outside perspective. Have you experienced being on auto-pilot when driving the same route day in and day out? Sometimes, we get to our destination and we don't remember the path we took to get there. Our lives can become a rutted routine when we are dealing with a wound. We internalize and seek only our own perspective because we are suffering. Our coping mechanisms become repetitive and we form unintentional habits. We need a fresh perspective to learn to separate from our emotions and see different vantage points.

How do we change how we view the event or trauma? We look at it like taking a different route home from work -from a new perspective. We pay more attention to details and become better aware of the experience. This subtle change in perspective can offer us freedom, bring us greater clarification, and allow us to set ourselves aside and explore the event through fresh eyes. Journal prompts at the end of this chapter will help draw out some of the viewpoints.

We need to be open to seeing the event or wounding from God's point of view. Using scripture, prayer and stories throughout the Bible, we should find God's perspective on what happened. We may not find the answers we are expecting. Looking at it as Jesus would may or may not shed light on a Divine purpose, but we will never know unless we seek His point of view.

CLARIFY

We must be clear on how we have handled our wounding. Understanding oneself is a journey within the larger path. We must find courage to get to the root of the painful problem. What coping mechanisms have we used along the way? Does our coping impact others? What is hindering our healing progress? These are some of the questions we must ask ourselves to gain clarity.

Gaining clarification on God's plan for us to sufficiently heal is the other aspect of this step. How does God see our wounding? What plan does He have in store for our sufficient healing? What does God has to say about all of this? What skills will God ask us to learn to achieve the next level of healing? Clarification on what God wants for us requires us to seek His presence, His purpose, and His perspective. We accomplish this through the two-way relationship we are creating with Him in prayer, reading scripture, and refocusing our thoughts on Him.

ASK

There is value in asking for constructive criticism, yet this may come with some discomfort. Asking others for opinions may elicit bad advice, a biased outlook based on their own experiences, and unproductive conversations. Or we may receive the best advice ever spoken. As we discussed, everyone is walking through life with their own wounds and are at various stages of healing – from none to sufficiently healed. We end up sharing our wounds, just as the lame man did, with those who offer no real help and are struggling.

Asking for help from experts is the right path to follow. Who knows us better than our Creator? Who understands the most intricate aspects of human psychology more than Jesus? This is our first step. Sometimes asking for professional help is crucial. Thomas needed help with his unbelief and he received no resolution from the disciples, his closest friends. He received what he needed from Christ Himself, the irrefutable, unmistakable truth.

According to Psychology Today, there are five reasons we need to seek therapy from a licensed therapist or psychologist.
1. Uncontrollable sadness, anger, or hopelessness;
2. Coping with substances or behavior to help us feel better;
3. Grief from the loss of a relationship, job, or multiple losses;
4. A history of being subjected to trauma, neglect, or abuse;
5. We cannot enjoy or stopped doing activities we like because painful emotions and experiences are getting in the way. [2]

Asking for help is a major step on the path to sufficient healing. Asking God to guide us means we are trusting in His plan. Communing with Him daily ensures a two-way relationship is developing. Asking for professional help when red flags pop up means we are taking responsibility for our actions and our role in healing our wounds into scars.

[2] 5 Signs It's Time to Seek Therapy. (n.d.). Retrieved from https://www.psychologytoday.com/us/blog/where-science-meets-the-steps/201303/5-signs-its-time-seek-therapy

REBUILD

Rebuilding oneself requires a plan, which we will address in the last chapter of this workbook. Just as the disciples had to rebuild their faith in Jesus, so do we need to rebuild ourselves according to God's plan. We do this by separating ourselves from the event, relationship or trauma, seek clarification on what God has laid out for our healing, and ask for help when we hit roadblocks along the way.

A rebuilding takes the pieces of ourselves we have hidden and brings them to the surface for scrutiny – we must undergo an assessment, a deep understanding of who we are and then who God says we are – His Beloved Child. We must fix those aspects of ourselves that do not fit into this definition. We need the tools, knowledge, and guidance to rebuild ourselves into the Beloved.

share

Telling the world our truth is powerful. It can bring about healing and change and give purpose and meaning behind what happened to us. Sharing our story needs to happen empathetically and respectfully to offer hope and encouragement to others.

We need to be at a place of sufficient healing, have courage, and offer purposeful truth. We should share our take on the healing process and encourage others desperate to move forward. We must show a roadmap of our healing journey, so others can see a template of their own map.

We must have resolution to our trauma, our wounding and show a life rebuilt. The lessons we learn along the way offer us a purpose behind the tragedy. Practice speaking, making a video or audio recording. This allows us a level of comfort and assuredness we will share the story with love, compassion, and truth.

THE QUESTIONS:

1. Identify the emotion, event or person on which you want to gain a different perspective?

_____

_____

_____

_____

_____

_____

2. What one thing needs God's clarification in your life?

_____

_____

_____

_____

_____

_____

_____

3. What aspect of yourself would you ask God to heal and why?

_____

_____

_____

_____

_____

_____

4. What tools do you foresee that may be useful in your healing journey?

_____

_____

_____

_____

_____

_____

5. Once your healing is sufficient and you have a full story to share, how will you convey it to others?

_____

_____

_____

_____

_____

_____

THE JOURNAL PROMPTS

Write from the other side – try writing techniques like persona poetry, fictional writing from the offender's perspective, or as a neutral third party. Have courage.

Write about what you have used to cope with the pain or unresolved issues from the wounding? Is it relational, chemical, emotional? How has the coping affected you and others?

Write about the event or relationship as a children's book telling details in the most simplistic form. What does the simple version offer you?

Journal freely on what life would be after the healing is complete? How do you think? What do your relationships look like? What changes do you foresee in yourself?

What is God's role in this healing journey? What questions do you have for Him? Use prayer and scripture to see His guidance

Chapter 3
Self-Assessment

MEDITATION – CONTEMPLATIVE PRAYER
Spend three minutes in silence focusing on one word to draw our attention back to God, Christ, Love or another powerful word to connect our spirit with the Holy.

THE STORY: Peter's Redemption
How does God view us? How do we see ourselves? Do we value who we are, or do we find our worth in comparing ourselves to others? When we examine ourselves and self-image, what do we discover? Do our thoughts reflect how God sees us or are we focused people's opinion? Jesus understood human nature and taught the disciples how much he valued them. Some did not see their worth even when Jesus told them repeatedly.

After the Resurrection, Jesus spent time with His disciples getting each one ready for their lifelong ministry in sharing the Gospel. Peter was a special case. In the Book of John, it shows us the redemption story of Peter after he denied knowing Jesus. He was the one disciple who walked on water (Matthew 14:29). He was the first disciple to declare Jesus the Son of God and Messiah with no one telling him so (Matthew 16:16). Peter then, as Jesus foresaw, denied knowing Christ during his arrest.

The redemption story began after Jesus and the disciples finished a meal. Jesus said to Peter, "Simon son of John, do you love me more than these?" (John 21:15) Jesus did not want a comparison of Peter's love for him versus the love of his fellow disciples and how they felt about Jesus. This was not Jesus' concern. He wanted to know if Peter loved Jesus – did Peter love the Messiah more than anyone, more than other people, family, friends, and fellow believers?

Peter responded "Yes, Lord. You know I love you." And Jesus gives Peter his first redemptive instruction, "Feed my lambs." (John 21:15)

Again, Jesus said, "Simon son of John, do you love me?" Peter answered, "Yes, Lord, you know that I love you." A second redemptive directive, Jesus said, "Take care of my sheep." (John 21:16)

The third time Jesus asked Peter, "Simon son of John, do you love me?" Peter found it hurtful Jesus would ask him three times and responded, "Lord, you know all things; you know I love you." Jesus gave the third instruction, "Feed my sheep." (John 21:17)

Jesus then gave Peter insight into the hardships of his ministry and foreshadowing of Peter's death. "Very truly I tell you, when you were younger you dressed yourself and went where you wanted; but when you are old you will stretch out your hands, and someone else will dress you and lead you where you do not want to go." Then Jesus said, "Follow me!" (John 21:18-19)

Peter turned and saw John, the same disciple considered Jesus' favorite and most loved. When Peter saw him, he asked, "Lord, what about him?" (John 21:20)

Jesus responded, "If I want him to remain alive until I return, what is that to you? You must follow me." John then explains rumors emerged over this statement, indicating he may never die; however, this was not true. Jesus' remarks were stating it was none of Peter's business what Jesus did or didn't do for the other disciples. (John 21:22-23)

What was Peter thinking? Did he not realize what just happened in this conversation with his Savior? Jesus reinstated him as Christ's disciple, a full redemption for the thrice denial which occurred a few weeks prior. Peter deemed leader of the flock, the Rock on which Jesus would build the church. (Matthew 16:18) Jesus even had Peter focus on Him rather than the disciples – "Do you love me more than these?" Am I the first one in your heart, Peter? Do I hold your love above all others? (John 21:15).

Peter focused on John, the Messiah's favorite (John 21:20). At least in Peter's opinion and likely John's, he was the favorite – John was the one who sat beside Jesus at the Passover Supper, leaned on Him and asked, "Lord, who will betray you?" (John 21:20). As soon as Peter saw John, his mind went straight to, "Well, what about him?" This shows Peter's level of insecurity although Jesus had just given him the template for caring for and directing the Church and knowledge of Peter's own death. As if Peter said, "I know what you said, Lord, but is John going to have it as hard as me? Is his death going to be as painful? And how much work will he have to do? Is he going to get a round questioning, too?"

"Yeah, yeah, yeah. I get what you're saying, but what about him?" was Peter's response. Do we feel like that sometimes? Feel like God gives others a better life, less pain, bigger house, more loving spouse, a healthier body? What about them, Lord, what about them? Why do they have it so good and I don't? This is normal human behavior, but not how God sees us. God doesn't love us more than others. He loves us without measure. There is no level of comparison.

THE LESSON: God-Assessment

God's assessment of us is a template all of us can use to determine how much God loves us. Are we ready to hear this? Do we want to know? God so loved – God so loved us, you, me – that He gave us His Son. All of us. We see this collectively but need to impose this individually.

Let us say this verse out loud – interjecting our name as if it were about us – in John 3:16-17, the verse states: "For God so loved the world that he gave his one and only Son, that whoever believes in him shall not perish but have eternal life. For God did not send his Son into the world to condemn the world, but to save the world through him."

Let us write our names in place of "the world" and "whoever". For God so loved _____ that he gave his one and only Son, that if _____ believes in him, he/she shall not perish but have eternal life. For God did not send his Son into the world to condemn _____, but to save _____ through him."

THE SKILL: Self-Talk

How do we talk to ourselves? Do we practice self-love or self-loath? If we had a friend who talked to us the way we talk to ourselves, would we be friends long? Our own self view may differ greatly from God's view of us. We are His Beloved Children, yet there are many times during the day in which we may talk to ourselves. This is unhealthy and can be detrimental to our wellbeing.

According to Dr. Dave Miers, manager for mental health services at Bryan Medical Center in Lincoln, NE and a founder and co-chair of the Nebraska State Suicide Prevention Coalition, negative self-talk is hurting us more than we know. Whether positive or negative thoughts, playing in our head, we develop filters. The filters influence how we view our reality. [3]

The article names one of the filters *The Emotional Reasoning Filter*[3] – meaning we may feel emotions in a situation having nothing to do with our current reality. When we self-criticize, we may isolate ourselves from others. We may think others feel about us the way we feel about ourselves. This mindset can affect our jobs, school, friends and family relationships.

To change *self-loath* to *self-love*, we need to find those negative judgements haunting us and change our thoughts. Being *aware* of our negative view is half the battle. The other part of the challenge is to replace the negative views with positive re-framing. Scriptures show us how valuable we are to God and will replace our negative thinking with focused repetition.

Physical things we can do to counter negativity include eating a balanced diet, surround ourselves with positive people, exercise, get a good night's sleep and practice deep breathing and positive self-imagery. We can also use self-affirmations - positive statements about ourselves as each negative habitual thought pops up. We need to be cheerleaders – "Way to go. You are doing great! You've got this!" is so much better than self-defeating talk.

[3] Miers, D., MD. (2018, July 16). Negative Self Talk: Is It Hurting You More Than You Know? Retrieved July 17, 2018, from https://www.bryanhealth.com/about-bryan-health/news/2018/-negative-self-talk-is-it-hurting-you-more-than-you-know/

THE QUESTIONS:

1. Name one negative thought you have about yourself. How would you feel if a friend described you that way? A stranger? When do you have these thoughts?

_____

_____

_____

_____

_____

2. Write ten positive words describing yourself.

_____

_____

_____

_____

_____

_____

3. How do you believe God sees you? How has He shown you how recently much He loves you?

_____

_____

_____

_____

_____

_____

_____

4. What scripture best describes the Love God has for you?

_____

_____

_____

_____

_____

_____

_____

5. Name three things you can do to change how you view yourself and be more aligned with how God views you.

_____

_____

_____

_____

_____

_____

_____

THE JOURNAL PROMPTS

Write an apology letter to yourself for thinking negative thoughts and explain what you will do to change your ways.

Write a love letter from God describing all things God loves about you.

Focus on one description of yourself, positive or negative, and discover when you began thinking that way and why.

Write a letter to yourself at the moment of wounding and offer words of encouragement hope.

As negative thoughts come, write them down. Acknowledge each and replace the negative thoughts with positive ones and scriptures countering each.

Chapter 4
The Heart of the Matter

MEDITATION – CONTEMPLATIVE PRAYER
Spend four minutes in silence focusing on one word to draw our attention back to God, Christ, Love or other powerful word to connect our spirit with the Holy.

THE STORY: Martha's Heart
In the previous chapter, Peter worried and compared John's instructions to his own. Why was Peter so focused on John after Jesus, the Son of God, had a deep, intimate, open conversation with him about his ministry and life? Sometimes we have been so wounded we focus on what others think of us, what others are doing, saying, being - we lose sight of ourselves in our wounding and forget who we are – God's Beloved. On the day Jesus came to have dinner, Martha was in such a struggle.

In the Book of Luke, Chapter 10, he shares with us the time Jesus and the disciples stopped in at the home of Martha and Mary. Martha invited them all to stay and started preparing for the guests. Martha's sister, Mary, however, was not helping with the household duties of cleaning, cooking and readying the accommodations. Instead, Mary sat at the feet of Jesus listening to what He was saying. (Luke 10:38).

Martha busied herself with preparing her home for the large group. She became distracted and she went to Jesus somewhat indignant, "Lord, don't you care that my sister has left me to do the work by myself? Tell her to help me!" Martha demanded. Martha's solution was to pull Mary away from Jesus, so she could help with the work. Then, Martha would have peace and not be distraught. (Luke 10:40)

Jesus had a different view of Martha's demand. "Martha, Martha," the Lord answered, "you are worried and upset about many things, but I need few things— or really only one. Mary has chosen what is better, and I will not take away it from her." (Luke 10:41-42) Jesus did not need Martha's preparation, her work, her checklist, no. He wanted for her the same as what He had offered Mary, a relationship with Him. Mary had chosen this closeness, to dwell in His presence, and remain focused on Christ. Martha had no time for a relationship.

Jesus showed Martha her incorrect thoughts. She was worried and upset about many things – she worried a lot! But it required only one thing of Martha – *to be with Jesus*. Mary made this choice from the moment Jesus arrived, while Martha labored in her worry. Haven't we all pointed the finger at someone or something else to deter the focus from ourselves? Or fixated on what we thought was important, while losing sight of what matters most? Jesus knew this about Martha and confronted her with, "Martha, Martha, why do you worry so much?"

Martha had a household of strangers to feed and it overwhelmed her. She was the one who asked the group to stay, but when she did, she knew she could count on Mary to help. When she spotted Mary just sitting, Martha turned to Jesus and ask Him to make her sister, Mary, get up and help. Jesus' solution was to point out the error in her mindset. *Relax, Martha, just be with Me.*

Martha wanted Jesus to make her sister conform to what she thought was right. Jesus let her know her idea of the right thing was *not* His. The *one thing* for Mary and Martha was to focus their mind and purpose on Him. It was all He required from each - nothing more. The lesson Jesus gave to Martha ties in with what Jesus shared with his disciples. "Don't worry about anything," Jesus explained. (Matthew 6:25). There is no need for worry about what to eat or drink, about the body, what to wear, or even about our lives. "But seek first his kingdom and his righteousness, and all these things will be given to you." Jesus directed the disciples. (Matthew 6:33) Seeking only God's Kingdom, at the feet of Jesus, is all He asked, and the daily tasks were not worth worrying over, they would take care of themselves.

Mary listened at Jesus' feet. Martha did things and then worried over them – she was torturing herself with things that didn't matter to Jesus. What was the heart of the matter? Martha was so focused on *doing* all the things she thought were valuable that she missed the precious moments of hearing the Messiah's words and being in His presence. Jesus wanted Martha's heart, not her work. Jesus knew the heart of the matter for Martha and showed it to her – a loving, but firm reproach from the Lord.

THE LESSON: God's Reproach

What is the heart of the matter? Do we distract ourselves with daily living, others, work, family, to mask what God wants us to focus on? What would we hear had we been Mary sitting at the feet of Jesus? Why was Martha worried in the first place? Was she in charge of the household? Did she have to step in to be the "parent" in place of her own? What was her wound and how did it cause her to react the way she did with her sister?

God will guide us to focus on Him and He knows we will, at times, get distracted with worldly things. Jesus reminds us with the two greatest commandments – "Love the Lord your God with all your heart and with all your soul and with all your mind and with all your strength. The second is this: Love your neighbor as yourself. There is no commandment greater than these." (Mark 12:30-31)

When we fall outside of these two commandments, we should expect God's reproach. The focus should always remain on Him and to show the same Love He has for us to others – as we love ourselves. When we are reminded of God's Love for us, the love we should have for ourselves should be easy – then we can see others in a different light and view them as God's Beloved Children as well.

THE SKILL: Getting to the Heart of the Matter (A Root Cause Analysis)

The root cause of any situation requires us to dig in, dig down and unearth the true reason for something – what happened, how it happened, why it happened, and finally, what needs to be corrected. [4]

We will use these methods to help us understand our own "heart of the matter". Let's do a Root Cause Analysis on Martha and see what we come up with using the components of the S.C.A.R.s Method:

[4] The Importance of Root Cause Analysis During Incident Investigation. (2016, October). Retrieved July 13, 2018, from https://www.osha.gov/Publications/OSHA3895.pdf United States Department of Labor OSHA - Ref DOC FS-3895 10/2016

Separate: Look at the storyline with Martha, Mary and Jesus. Talk through the events that took place from beginning to end.

Clarify: Martha was stressed out and worried over preparing for the guests. Let's try to figure out why – ask why five times and see what is revealed.

Rebuild: What could Martha have done to avoid being stressed out and distraught? What actions could Martha have taken in the future to keep from worrying or being distraught in similar situations? Based on the investigation of Martha and the event, write down the Heart of the Matter:

_____

_____

_____

_____

What about our own wounding? When we look at our trauma/event/wounding as a case study, separating our emotions as that of a third person as we do Martha's situation, what do we find? We should find clarity in what is the heart of the matter – what is the one thing we have carried in our wounding needing the most attention? What is the one thing God is showing us needs to change, or be set aside? Let us be courageous, go through the process of discovery, and see what is revealed.

_____

_____

_____

_____

THE QUESTIONS:

1. Describe the event/wounding/problem – try to answer the question why at least five times.

_____

_____

_____

_____

_____

_____

2. Write a timeline of the event/wounding/problem – what happened and when.

_____

_____

_____

_____

_____

_____

3. From your perspective, what could you have done to change, prevent, or keep the wounding from happening again?

_____

_____

_____

_____

_____

_____

4. What is the one thing you have struggled with since the event/wounding/problem?

_____

_____

_____

_____

_____

_____

5. What would God's advice be for your heart of the matter?

_____

_____

_____

_____

_____

_____

_____

THE JOURNAL PROMPTS

Make a list of the top ten traumatic events you have experienced and whittle down the list to the one you believe has affected you the most.

Describe the event/ wounding/ problem as if it had a different outcome. What changes did you make in the timeline or story to have a different outcome? What does that change mean to you?

Pick a feeling or emotion you wrestle with often and draw out the current circumstances around the feeling. When do you feel this way? Why do you feel this way? Keep asking why until you find the heart of the matter.

Write down action items to help you deal with the emotions, negative feelings, and draw you closer to God. Pick the one thing you know would help you the most. What can you do to keep yourself focused on this one helpful thing?

Chapter 5
The Boundaries

MEDITATION – CONTEMPLATIVE PRAYER
Spend five minutes in silence focusing on one word to draw our attention back to God, Christ, Love or other powerful word to connect our spirit with the Holy.

THE STORY: Jesus' Boundaries
We all need healthy boundaries in our relationships, marriage, friendships, family relations and to help us have control of our lives. Wounding interferes with boundaries. The less we value ourselves, the fewer boundaries we will put in place. When we set boundaries and others attempt to violate the parameters, we need to maintain control either through reminding others, or through removing ourselves from the situation. As best-selling author and psychologist Henry Cloud said in *Boundaries in Marriage*, "You get what you tolerate."

Jesus set boundaries throughout His life and ministry to stay focused on His purpose and fulfill God's plan. He often spent time in prayer. Sometimes, when it was still dark outside, and he would leave to go to a private place and pray. (Mark 1:35) Other times, Jesus would head to a mountainside and devote the whole night praying to God. Most times, as He did just before His arrest, Jesus went to the Mount of Olives to pray. (Luke 22:39-42)

Jesus kept focused on His purpose regardless of what others said. He was assertive not only with the Jewish leaders, but also His disciples. When Jesus predicted His death, Peter spoke up and said, "That will never happen to you, Lord." Jesus put Peter in his place. Jesus said, "Get behind me, Satan! You are a stumbling block to me; you do not have in mind the concerns of God, but merely human concerns." (Matthew 16:22-23) Jesus knew the fear Peter had and his concern over his future, but there was no time for Peter's way of thinking. Jesus would let nothing, or no one impede the events set in motion by God. His boundaries were clear.

Jesus gave explicit instructions to the disciples on what they needed to do to be His followers. "Whoever wants to be my disciple must deny themselves and take up their cross and follow me. For whoever wants to save their life will lose it, but whoever loses their life for me will find it." (Matthew 16:24-25, Mark 8:33-35) He also offered boundaries for the disciples to follow in case they met communities of people who would not listen to the message. "And if any place will not welcome you or listen to you, leave that place and shake the dust off your feet as a testimony against them." (Matthew 10:14, Mark 6:11, Luke 9:5)

During Jesus' ministry, not only did He set clear boundaries for the disciples, He set concise boundaries with His family. In Mark Chapter 3, we learn not only the teachers of the law were questioning Him, but Jesus' family also. When Jesus and the disciples entered a house, a large crowd gathered. Jesus' family heard about it and thought Jesus had lost His mind. They went to "take charge of him." When Jesus' mother and brothers arrived, they stood outside the house and asked someone to call for Jesus. Word passed through the crowd and Jesus heard His mother and brothers were looking for Him. (Mark 3:20-21,31-32)

Jesus' response was "Who are my mother and my brothers?" He glanced at the crowd of people in the house and said, "Here are my mother and my brothers! Whoever does God's will is my brother and sister and mother." Jesus neither dispersed the crowd nor went out to meet His mother and brothers. He was doing God's work and despite His family's opinion, He would continue to minister to those gathered around Him and beyond. (Mark 3:33-35)

Jesus knew what His family was up to and did not allow them to interrupt what He was doing. He knew the work God set before Him and He let nothing impede fulfilling God's will. He not only set the boundaries for His family members, He redefined family all together – those doing God's work. That was His family. Whether it was direct or indirect, Jesus set the boundaries for His family to be in His life – do God's work and you are in, stand in the way of God's plan and you are out. To Jesus, it was simple – boundaries had to be set and kept.

THE LESSON: God's Take on Boundaries

God has given people clear expectations and boundaries from the beginning. Adam and Eve had one boundary – do not eat the fruit of the tree in the garden's middle – both disobeyed and suffered the consequences. (Genesis 3:1-20) Moses received instructions from God to take the staff, gather the people, and *speak* to the rock to bring forth water. Moses disobeyed and struck the rock with the staff instead of following God's instructions – it cost Moses entrance into the Holy Land. (Numbers 20:2-13) Jonah was to go to the city of Ninevah to preach against its wickedness – Jonah ran away to Tarshish instead. Jonah spent three days in the belly of a whale. (Jonah 1:1-3,17)

God sets boundaries for us to fulfill His purpose and become the person He created us to be. He loves us and wants us with Him always. Boundaries are part of what keeps us close to Him and in His presence. The ten commandments were the boundaries for His people. Jesus narrowed the ten down to two – Love God, love others as you love yourself. Anything outside of these is outside of God's boundaries for us.

THE SKILL: Boundaries – Set It and Don't Forget It

To set and keep boundaries, we must first discover and decide when our boundaries are crossed. Once we discover our boundaries, we must communicate these with those around us and with expectations of changing ourselves. We must keep our boundaries even as they are challenged. The better we know ourselves as God's Beloved Child, the better we identify what matters, set clear boundaries, and maintain strong standards. Let's look at developing the boundaries we need to set through the S.C.A.R.s. Method® (minus the sharing portion):

SEPARATE: We need to separate ourselves from those that cause us pain and turmoil – emotionally and sometimes physically. Keep in mind as we set our boundaries, we will not be doing this to change the behavior of others, we will set and keeping boundaries to change our own expectations of how we are treated. Separating ourselves from someone who physically harms us should be immediate and with legal backup. We should never tolerate physical abuse and law it may require enforcement to make the separation safe and effective.

Separating from those who are berating us verbally, psychologically or emotionally requires a clear understanding of what is acceptable and unacceptable to us. Valuing ourselves, as God values us, allows us to set emotion aside and look at the situation with new eyes and an open heart. When someone lies to us, how do we react and feel? How about when others criticize or make fun of us? Do we accept this is *just how they are* and move on? Do we feel hurt or harmed, but take no action? Do we laugh it off as a joke, but feel the sting deep inside? Or do we react by yelling and berating the person in hopes they get the message?

We may be challenged to keep our emotions separate from the issue, but we can do this by asking, "Would God do or say that to me?" If the answer is no, there is a clear breach of boundaries. As we gain the skills of setting and keeping boundaries, we will expect others to treat us as we treat ourselves, as God's Beloved Child.

CLARIFY: Do we have someone close to us who violates our boundaries? There are several ways boundaries can be crossed. Let's go through some scenarios to understand what violations may look like and what boundaries we need in place. There are different boundary violations, according to Psychology Today: [5]

- Verbal - When someone verbally violates our boundaries, they may yell at us, cut us off, say inflammatory things, or gossip about us. These are ways others cross the boundaries of being in a healthy friendship or relationship.
- Psychological/Emotional – When someone lies to us, demeans or criticizes us, or tries to make us feel guilty about our thoughts, beliefs or emotions, it violates boundaries. Any bullying, embarrassment, or shaming is also a boundary violation.
- Physical – This boundary is more than physical abuse. It also includes subtle violations like standing too close, invading our personal space, touching us without permission, being inappropriate, destroying our property, and violating our privacy.

- [5] Brenner, A., MD. (2015, November 21). 7 Tips to Create Healthy Boundaries with Others. Retrieved August 12, 2018, from https://www.psychologytoday.com/us/blog/in-flux/201511/7-tips-create-healthy-boundaries-others

ASK:

Expressing what we expect from those who are boundary breakers may be difficult at first. As we set and keep boundaries, we gain control and bring our power back where it belongs - within ourselves. We must set where our boundaries are and why they matter. Here is the kicker, however – others still may not comply. We need to believe what we say is final, set and clear – regardless of how others react, what they feel, or believe.

Asking those closest to us to help in setting boundaries requires trust. When we are clear, provide a reason behind the purpose, and continue to keep boundaries set, our relationships will improve. It may never change the other person; however, the changes in us will reset the relationship with little or no effort on their end. It may even inspire others to look at their own boundaries and expectations. Our focus is to ask those in our lives to honor and respect our boundaries as we see fit to set and keep them.

REBUILD:
We must know, take responsibility, and develop a respect for the ourselves, God's Beloved Child. When we view ourselves as the Beloved, our standards rise to a higher level. The respect we have for ourselves increases as we rediscover how much God values us as His Children. The rebuilding portion of boundary setting means we rebuild ourselves – not someone else.

We must never assume setting boundaries will ever change someone else's behavior. Sometimes it may require difficult choices in who is in our life or how much time we spend with certain people. We cannot fix others. We can't – and waste a lifetime trying to do just that. Or we allow others to overstep boundaries for various reasons – to not be alone, to accepted by them, to be a part of their lives, to feel validated or loved. None of these are acceptable reasons for narrowing or diminishing our boundaries.

God's love for us is immense, passionate, and radical. The closer we are to Him, the less we tolerate abuse and manipulation from others. God redefines us through Christ – we must, therefore, redefine how others treat us. Those who value healthy relationships will accept the boundaries and respect our wishes for what *we establish* to be good and right. Boundaries show the world we no longer accept the unacceptable. Boundaries say, "I value myself and am in charge of how I am treated." Others will follow or not.

share:

Sharing before sufficient healing occurs may turn into a dumping session with our friends and loved ones to unburden ourselves of the trauma we have endured. Seeking the advice and help from a professional counselor or therapist is where sharing before healing is acceptable. We must share *only* after sufficient healing occurs and in situations in which our story will provide hope and encouragement to others on their path to healing.

THE QUESTIONS:

1. Thinking about the heart of the matter in Chapter 4 – what person, situation or reoccurring event should be tested for boundary setting? What type of violation is happening? Verbal, psychological/emotional, or physical?

_____

_____

_____

_____

_____

2 What red flag warnings should you look out for during this situation? What boundaries do you need to set when warnings arise?

_____

_____

_____

_____

_____

3 Write down one situation in which an established boundary is needed now. What steps do you need to take to set and keep the boundary? (start small if needed)

_____

_____

_____

_____

_____

_____

_____

4   What does your life look like with boundaries in place?

---

5   Find one scripture that gives you courage to set and keep boundaries with
    those closest to you.

THE JOURNAL PROMPTS

Write about a scenario – real world or fictional – in which a boundary is clearly violated – describe what type, red flag warnings, and your verbal and physical response to the violations.

How should others speak to us? Journal of others who do not speak to you as you wish and write out a dialog to ask them to honor your newly set boundaries. What steps will you take to ensure the boundary is set and kept?

What steps should you take to ensure others see the boundaries you have set for yourself? Verbally, physically, psychological/emotionally?

Think of one person who has overstepped boundaries in your life and you missed the opportunity to establish and set boundaries with them. Who was it, what did they do, and how would you handle the situation differently?

Make a list of rules – boundary rules you set for yourself – and keep the list going as you find more that need to be put into place.

Chapter 6
Difficult Conversations

MEDITATION – CONTEMPLATIVE PRAYER
Spend six minutes in silent prayer focusing on one word to draw our attention back to God, Christ, Love or other powerful word to connect our spirit with the Holy.

THE STORY: Jesus' Conversation with Nicodemus
When we contemplate having a difficult conversation, anxiety ensues. How will the other person react? What will they say? How will I say what I mean without getting emotional? Our thoughts muddle and tongue ties when the conversation deals with our wounding. Conversations will challenge us regardless of where we are in the healing process and even when we are sufficiently healed. Let's read how Jesus handled difficult conversations.

In the Book of John Chapter 3, Jesus sat down with the Pharisee, Nicodemus, in one of the most important conversations of His ministry. Nicodemus was a member of the Jewish ruling council, a scholar, and educated. He visited at night to have a private conversation with Jesus. Nicodemus opened the discussion by offering who he thought Jesus was – a great teacher who has come from God. (John 3:1-3)

Jesus responded by laying the groundwork for one of the most important statements He would ever make. "No one can see the kingdom of God unless they are born again," Jesus replied. Nicodemus questioned how this could be? How could one be born a second time from his mother? (John 3:3-4)

Jesus explains His meaning is one of spirit not of body, one must be reborn of water and Spirit. Then Jesus challenged Nicodemus, "You should not be surprised at my saying, 'You must be born again.'" Nicodemus still not understanding, asked how one can be born again of the spirit. (John 3:5-9)

Again, Jesus reproaches Nicodemus, "You are Israel's teacher, and you still don't understand these things?" Jesus continued saying they, He and the disciples, had given testimony, offered what the group had seen and knew to be true, yet the Jewish leaders would not accept their words as truth. Nicodemus was the representative of the Jewish ruling council and was a member of the teachers who did not believe Jesus and His followers. None the less, Jesus laid out the truth in front of him and seized on the opportunity to speak the truth we still talk about today. (John 3:10-12)

That night, as Nicodemus sat with Jesus in close conversation, he was front row to hear the most profound statements from the Messiah Himself. Jesus declared He was the Son of Man and foreshadowed His resurrection and purpose – "that everyone who believes may have eternal life in him." (John 3:13-15) He also revealed why God sent Him to this world, what Christ's purpose was, and what it means to believe in Him and be His follower. (John 3:16-21)

Nicodemus was the first person to hear *John 3:16* – Jesus spoke the truth of who He to the only teacher who dared come speak with Him. Did this conversation impact Nicodemus? In Chapters 7 we hear Nicodemus defending Jesus in front of the Pharisees as they berated the temple guards for not bringing Jesus in – Nicodemus defended, "Does our law condemn a man without first hearing him to find out what he has been doing?" (John 7:51)

Nicodemus then partners with Joseph of Arimathea, who asked Pilate for Jesus' body after the crucifixion. Nicodemus brought seventy-five pounds of myrrh and aloes. He helped Joseph of Arimathea wrap Jesus' body with spices and strips of linen as required by Jewish burial customs. (John 19:38-40) Nicodemus was the one who laid Jesus' body to rest in the tomb. He was one of the last two people who saw Jesus' dead, wrapped body before the resurrection.

Imagine the learned Jewish leader going to visit Jesus at night to seek a conversation. What Nicodemus received was a life changing lesson from the Messiah.

THE LESSON: God's Conversations

God held many conversations throughout the Bible. God had a difficult conversation with Noah, "I am going to put an end to all people, for the earth is filled with violence because of them. I am surely going to destroy both them and the earth." (Genesis 6:13) What a profound and disturbing thing Noah heard. And then followed by - Oh by the way, go build an ark out of cypress for you, your family and animals I will send to you. (Genesis 6:14-21) What about the difficult conversation God had with Abraham telling him to sacrifice Isaac. (Genesis 22:2) Many times, God said profound things people did not want to hear or had a hard time comprehending.

In the New Testament, Jesus offered the disciples and followers the Holy Spirit. God communicates with us through the Holy Spirit when we are in communion with Him. The Holy Spirit will also give us the words to say during difficult conversations when we give our words over to God.

THE SKILL: Preparing for Difficult Conversations
SEPARATE:

The best method in preparing for a difficult conversation is to look at the other person's point of view. As mad as we may be with emotions emerging, seeing life from someone else's perspective is helpful in preparing for a difficult conversation. Each of us will interpret events, trauma and relationships from our own point of view, we must seek to understand the other point of view to have a productive, meaningful and healthy conversation. We need to work through selfish viewpoints and get ourselves to the point of *curiosity*.

CLARIFY:

Why have this conversation? Do we want to argue our point? Do we want to impose our side of the story? Do we want to unleash the negative emotions the other person dumped on us? Are they the problem and we want to let them know about it? Answering yes to any of these questions defeats the purpose for a constructive (yet difficult) conversation. We need to work through the negative emotions and views *first* before a conversation. If we view the other person as the problem, they may feel the same about us. We can use the Five-Why method to root out why we want to discuss an issue. Once this is complete, we need to be clear on the points we want to get across from the "I" perspective. When such and such happened, I felt_____. When you said this and that, I believed it to mean _____. We must have clarity going into a difficult conversation to prepare us to help the other person express themselves, and then they can better hear us.

ASK:

Just because we want to have a discussion doesn't mean the other person will accept the invitation. When we are prepared to hear their side of the story – yes, their side – our invitation must state that intention. We need to be up front about what it is we want to talk about and open the door for the other person to share – their feelings, their story, their side, their perspective. We must become superb at *listening.* An invitation asking someone to speak so we can listen is a powerful request. Most people will not turn that down. We must also be open and let the other person know we will share our feelings, that blame is not part of the discussion, and our purpose is to seek resolution or at the least an open forum to agree to disagree. We must honor our own feelings and be able to share those without blaming the other person.

REBUILD:

We can either use the difficult conversation to rebuild a lost or damaged relationship or not. Part of the rebuilding process when recovering from a wound is the ability to become a different person because of it. Having a difficult conversation with another constructively can be one of the most powerful litmus tests we can have to show how much we have grown and changed. The conversation may reunite us with someone or it may magnify how we have healed. We may find wounding no longer occurs.

For more instructions on these tough conversations, read "Difficult Conversations: How to Discuss What Matters Most" by Stone, Patton and Heen and "Boundaries Face to Face," by Dr. Henry Cloud and Dr. John Townsend.

1. Who do I need to have a discussion with and why?

_____

_____

_____

_____

_____

_____

_____

2. What is the best venue for this conversation? In person, on the phone? Email?

_____

_____

_____

_____

_____

_____

3 What questions should I ask the other person to have them share their side of the story?

_____

_____

_____

_____

_____

_____

4   What will I do to keep myself from reacting negatively when they share their perspective?

_____

_____

_____

_____

_____

_____

_____

5   What requests do I have of God during the preparation and actual conversation?

_____

_____

_____

_____

_____

_____

_____

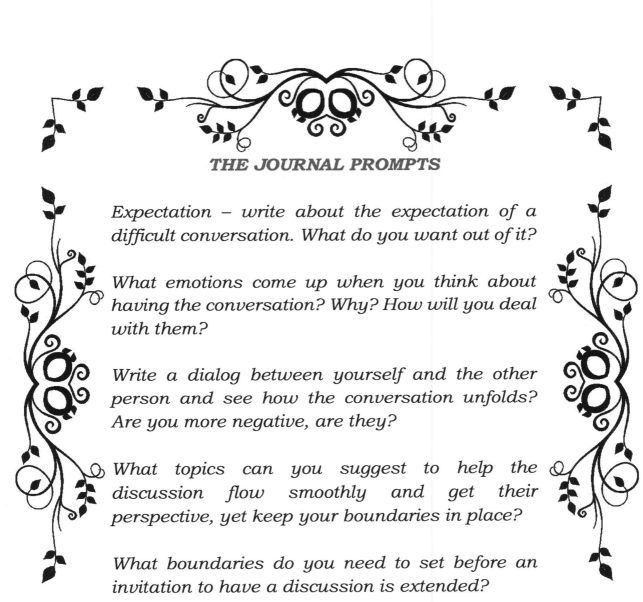

THE JOURNAL PROMPTS

Expectation – write about the expectation of a difficult conversation. What do you want out of it?

What emotions come up when you think about having the conversation? Why? How will you deal with them?

Write a dialog between yourself and the other person and see how the conversation unfolds? Are you more negative, are they?

What topics can you suggest to help the discussion flow smoothly and get their perspective, yet keep your boundaries in place?

What boundaries do you need to set before an invitation to have a discussion is extended?

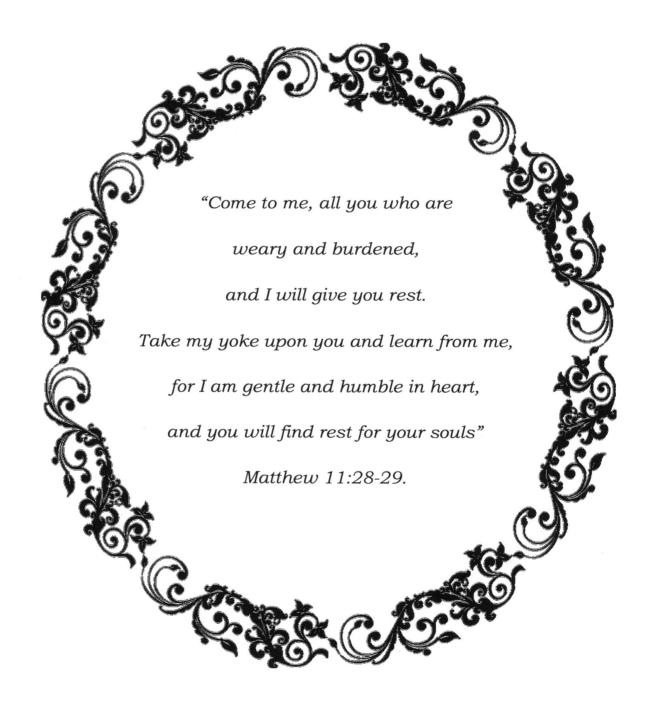

"Come to me, all you who are

weary and burdened,

and I will give you rest.

Take my yoke upon you and learn from me,

for I am gentle and humble in heart,

and you will find rest for your souls"

Matthew 11:28-29.

Chapter 7
Tending The Beloved

MEDITATION – CONTEMPLATIVE PRAYER
Spend seven minutes in silence focusing on one word to draw our attention back to God, Christ, Love or other powerful word to connect our spirit with the Holy.

THE STORY: Pruning the Dead & Fruitful
Are there things in our lives we know are not good for us, yet they linger? Bad habits, toxic relationships, or daily distractions from our relationship with God? What if we could just cut those parts out of our lives, like a gardener prunes a tree or plant? Jesus knows just how this is done and shares it with His disciples.

In John Chapter 15, Jesus tells His disciples He is the true vine, and God is the gardener. God will be the loving gardener and will remove every piece that does not bear fruit. Not only does God obliterate every branch that doesn't bear fruit, He prunes those branches that bear fruit, so they will be even more fruitful. (John 15:1-2)

Jesus explains to the disciples they are already clean because of everything He has already told them. The disciples received instructions to remain in Jesus as He remains in them. The disciples cannot be fruitful unless they remain in Christ. (John 15:3-4)

Jesus is the vine, the disciples the branches and if they remain in Him and He in them, they will be fruitful. Without Jesus, the disciples can do nothing. Apart from Christ, the disciples will be like a branch tossed and withered. Those branches are thrown into the fire and burned. (John 15:5-6)

Just as God loves Jesus, Jesus loved them. He directed the disciples to remain in His love. If they remembered and kept Jesus' commands, the disciples would remain in His love, just as He kept God's commands and remained in His love.

Jesus continues to tell the disciples why He is telling them all of this – so that His joy may be in them and their joy would be complete. (John 15:9-11)

Jesus gives one command: Love each other as He loved them. The greatest love is "to lay down one's life for one's friends." Jesus called the disciples His friends and no longer servants, because of all the knowledge they had accumulated from everything God revealed to Jesus and He shared with them. (John 15:12-15)

Jesus finished by saying He chose the disciples and appointed them, so they may "go bear fruit – fruit that will last." Whatever the disciples ask of God in Jesus' name will be granted. Jesus reaffirmed, "This is my command: Love each other." (John 15:16-17)

THE LESSON: God the Gardener

God is the Master Gardener and knows what needs removing from our lives and what needs pruning. Lop off any bad stuff, nurture the good. One of the greatest examples is the Apostle Paul. God took one of the worst enemies of the early Christian church and transformed him, starting with the encounter with Christ on the road to Damascus. But God didn't stop there. He honed Paul's skills, used his talents, and took away all things not aligned with His grand plan of spreading the Gospel.

God will do the same for us. Jesus gave us the template for what to expect and our responsibility in the relationship in John Chapter 15. We are to remain in Him for Jesus is the vine – we are to tap into Him for all things, always, remain in Him. We are to love each other just as God loves each of us and rest in the joy only Christ can bring to us. And we too expect the Master Gardener to work on us, cut out the bad, prune the good – and tend to us, His Beloved Child.

THE SKILL: Let God Tend Us

Imagine we are a fruit tree. How do we look? Are we bearing fruit, being productive, doing God's will, working towards a healthy life, aiming for sufficient healing? Or do we have dead branches holding us back, fruitless, serving no purpose and zapping the energy necessary to do the fruitful things? We all find ourselves in need of pruning just as a fruit tree requires pruning to bear healthy fruit.

Let's talk about two things:
1. Dead Branches - Those things not serving us maintain a wounded state, are not fruitful and requires removal from our lives.
2. Proper Pruning – The aspects of ourselves needing a little tweaking for a more fruitful and healthier life.

Gardeners remove the dead branches and parts from a plant to keep it healthy. Keeping a dead branch on a tree can invite disease, insects, and damage. The dead branches for us are those things in our lives that keep us wounded and blocked from who God created us to be. Unhealthiness requires permanent removal – complete and forevermore. Once and for all, God wants to take the deadness from our lives and replace it with fruitfulness and joy.

Gardeners also prune to help plants become more fruitful by cutting out small portions of the vine or branch. There is no need to purge it, but one must cut away a percentage to divert energy to the fruitful portion of branch or vine. This increases the size and healthiness fruit. The same goes for us.

God wants to prune those things blocking our fruitfulness and holding us back from sufficient healing. He wants to fine tune the talent, relationship, job, or circumstance in our lives. He may give us a different perspective, change our attitude, or let us see circumstances from His view. Just a little pruning to make us more aligned with who He created us to be – His Beloved Child.

THE QUESTIONS:

1. What "dead branch" do you suspect God wants to remove from your life? Is it the same as the "Heart of the Matter" in Chapter 4? If not, how does this new revelation make you feel? If so, how can this "removal" help you?

---

2. What one thing in your life, habit, or attitude could use some of God's pruning? What steps can you take to help in the process?

---

3. How has your wounding affected the fruitful side of your life? With sufficient healing, what kind of fruit would you bear?

---

4. What steps can you take to "remain in Jesus" as He directed his disciples?

_____

_____

_____

_____

_____

_____

_____

5. Find a scripture supporting your healing process.

_____

_____

_____

_____

_____

_____

_____

THE JOURNAL PROMPTS

Imagine your life with the Joy of Jesus. What does that look like? How would it impact your healing process?

What kind of fruit tree would you be? And why did you choose this tree? What would you do to maintain the health of this tree? How does that apply to your own life?

What one bad habit, if removed, would transform your life?

What would you do with your life once that habit was removed?

What is the one most unproductive thing you dwell on or interferes with your healing? What scripture can you use to counter this "dead branch" in your thinking?

Chapter 8
Plan of Action

MEDITATION – CONTEMPLATIVE PRAYER
Spend eight minutes in silence focusing on one word to draw our attention back to God, Christ, Love or other powerful word to connect our spirit with the Holy.

THE STORY: Jesus Accepts Requests
So, what should we ask for in our healing process? What needs adjusting and tending to for sufficient healing? What aspects of ourselves need to change to move forward on our healing path? Clarity on your plan of action is essential for our healing process. Our words need careful crafting when asking God for these things. Jesus said in Matthew 7:7 Ask and I will give it to you, seek and you will find Me, knock and I'll open the door for you."

In the Book of Mark, Chapter 10, we read the unusual request from two of Jesus' disciples, James and John, the sons of Zebedee. The brothers requested Jesus do whatever they asked. Jesus responded by asking what it was the brothers wanted of Him. The two men replied with the lofty request of one brother sitting at His right and the other on His left in His Glory. Jesus said, *"You don't know what you are asking."* Could the men follow the path of Jesus, drink from the cup He drank from and become baptized as He was baptized? Why, yes, yes, they could follow all Jesus asked and more, they responded. (Mark 10:35-39)

Jesus let the brothers know they would follow His path, drink from the cup, and baptized just as He was – BUT to do what they requested, to sit at His right hand and His left, would not be granted. God prepared those seats for others. When fellow disciples heard of the brothers' request, it outraged them. Jesus gathered them all together to explain. (Mark 10:40-42)

Jesus said earthly rulers, those rulers of the Gentiles, raise themselves up and exercise authority over the people. Not so with the disciples, however, the hierarchy was reversed. Those who were greatest will be least and those who served others would be the greatest of all. Even the Son of Man was on the earth to serve and not be served, for His life would be the ransom for many.

This, likely, was not the answer James and John sought. What they were asking for and what they received were not the same. The two wanted to elevation to the highest level, and, once Jesus explained what that entailed, they assumed they were ready. However, their goal of being seated at Jesus' right and left was not the offering. Instead, Jesus explained their thoughts were not aligned with God's will and the plan of action differed greatly from their expectations. They would need to serve, so much so that whoever wanted to be first must become servant all. (Mark 10:44)

THE LESSON: God's Action Plan

God's plan did not meet the expectations of a few characters in the Old Testament either. The story of Joseph showed God's plan had many twists and turns involving the young man's kidnapping by his brothers and sale into slavery to the Midianites, then the ensuing sale to Potiphar, one of the Egyptian Pharaoh's officials. Joseph had to work hard, thwart plans against him, survive prison, and come to a place of power all to save God's chosen people and his family from starvation. (Genesis 37,39-50) Definitely not the plan Joseph had expected as the most beloved son of Jacob. His life of twists and turns, trials and triumphs were all part of God's plan for Joseph and His people.

God has a plan for each of us. It may not look like what we expect, but, through Christ, the plan will be revealed so we may fulfill His purpose and be the person He created us to be. Our request will be fulfilled through God's will for our lives. The outcome may not look like we envision. However, His plan is perfect, sufficient, and trustworthy. We must seek to find His plan and look at our healing path from His perspective.

THE SKILL: A Plan of Action

1. From Chapter 1, contemplate the one thing you believe God has shown you to achieve sufficient healing, but you have not had the courage to act? Is the one thing still the same? If yes, what steps has God shown you through this course to take to action on this "one thing"? If not, what is the new revelation God has shown you to achieve sufficient healing? What steps has He shown you to achieve this new path?

_____

_____

_____

_____

_____

_____

_____

2. From Chapter 2, what aspect of yourself would you ask God to heal? Has this changed during the course? If so, what is the new aspect you have found needs healing. If not, what has God revealed during the course to heal this portion of yourself?

_____

_____

_____

_____

_____

_____

_____

3. From Chapter 2, Name three things you can do to change how you view yourself and more align with God' views you. Of those three things from Chapter 2, which ones have you tried? Did they work?

----

4. What adjustments do you need to make, or do you need to write a whole new list?

----

5. From Chapter 4, what is the one thing you have struggled with since the event/wounding/problem? How have you dealt with this during the course? What changes are needed to not struggle with this anymore? What long-term plan do you have to get past it?

----

6. What has changed while taking this course about how you view the event/wounding/relationship different than before? How will that realization help you?

_____

_____

_____

_____

_____

_____

7. What has God shown you through this course that has impacted your life, self-image, relationships, and wounding?

_____

_____

_____

_____

_____

_____

_____

_____

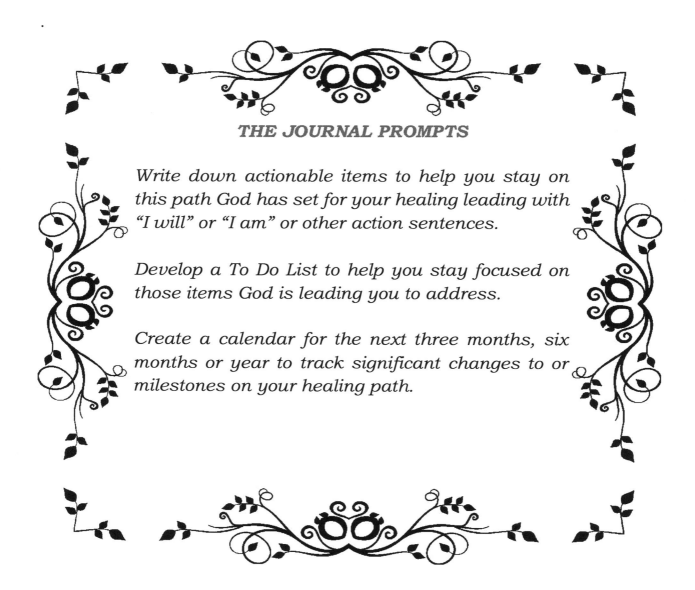

THE JOURNAL PROMPTS

Write down actionable items to help you stay on this path God has set for your healing leading with "I will" or "I am" or other action sentences.

Develop a To Do List to help you stay focused on those items God is leading you to address.

Create a calendar for the next three months, six months or year to track significant changes to or milestones on your healing path.

Action Planner

Action	How	When

Thought Planner

Negative Thought	Verse	Positive Thought

Journal

Chapter One

Chapter Two

Chapter Three

Chapter Four

Chapter Five

Chapter Six

Chapter Seven

Chapter Eight

RESOURCES

BOOKS:

Boundaries: When to Say Yes, How to Say No to Take Control of Your Life by Henry Cloud and John Townsend

Get Unstuck Now: How Smart People Gain Clarity and Solve a Problem Fast, And How You Can Too by Laura van den Berg Sekac

Difficult Conversations: How to Discuss What Matters Most by Douglas Stone and Bruce Patton

Boundaries Face to Face: How to Have That Difficult Conversation You've Been Avoiding How to Have That Difficult Conversation You've Been Avoiding by Henry Cloud and John Townsend

The Body Keeps the Score: Brain, Mind, and Body in the Healing of Trauma by Bessel van der Kolk M.D.

Healing from Hidden Abuse: A Journey Through the Stages of Recovery from Psychological Abuse by Shannon Thomas LCSW

Setting Boundaries with Your Adult Children: Six Steps to Hope and Healing for Struggling Parents by Allison Bottke

Setting Boundaries® with Difficult People: Six Steps to SANITY for Challenging Relationships by Allison Bottke and Karol Ladd

Get Personal: The Importance of Sharing Your Faith Story by Erin K. Casey

Improving Your Storytelling: Beyond the Basics for All Who Tell Stories in Work and Play by Doug Lipman

Telling Your Own Stories (American Storytelling) by Donald Davis

RESOURCES (cont'd)
COUNSELING SERVICES:

You may search these professional organizations for a counselor or therapist or contact your state's counseling association.

The American Association of Christian Counselors
https://www.aacc.net/

The American Mental Health Counselors Association
http://www.amhca.org/home

Contact your local church to see if there are confidential resources or referrals available in your area.

ABOUT THE AUTHOR

Michelle Andrea Williams, MBA, is an industry news writer for a healthcare analytics company and a member of the Non-Fiction Authors Association. She has written articles for healthcare industry journals and has decades of experience in business, employee training, and policy and procedure writing. Michelle is the co-founder and current board member of MBS4God International, Inc., a non-profit organization helping the poor and underserved around the world.

Michelle co-leads a women's group at her church and assists her husband Greg in teaching an Adult Sunday School class. Occasionally, she teaches small group sessions and leads retreats on various topics including healing from trauma, changing habits, and self-care. Michelle is many things to many people, but most of all, she is a beloved child of God who is forgiven, loved, ever-changing and made flawless through Jesus Christ.

Visit the author's website for more information: michelleandreawilliams.com

Made in the
USA
Lexington, KY